I SEE
(HEAR, TASTE, SMELL, AND TOUCH)
SANTA FE !

A Children's Guide

Libby Lynn and Moses James

Cleanan Press, Inc.
Santa Fe, NM

© Copyright 1989, 2019
by Lynn Michelsohn and Moses Michelsohn
ISBN: 978-1795762151
Print Edition 1.4 KDP (5/19)
Also available as an ebook
Cleanan Press, Inc.
663 Bishops Lodge Road
Santa Fe, NM 87501 USA

Cover Illustration: Gary Glasgow, Animated Images
Layout: Tadd Johnson

I see the **COLORS** of Santa Fe . . .

Santa Fe is built of **BROWN** adobe.
Adobe is the color of mud, because
adobe is made of mud, dried mud.

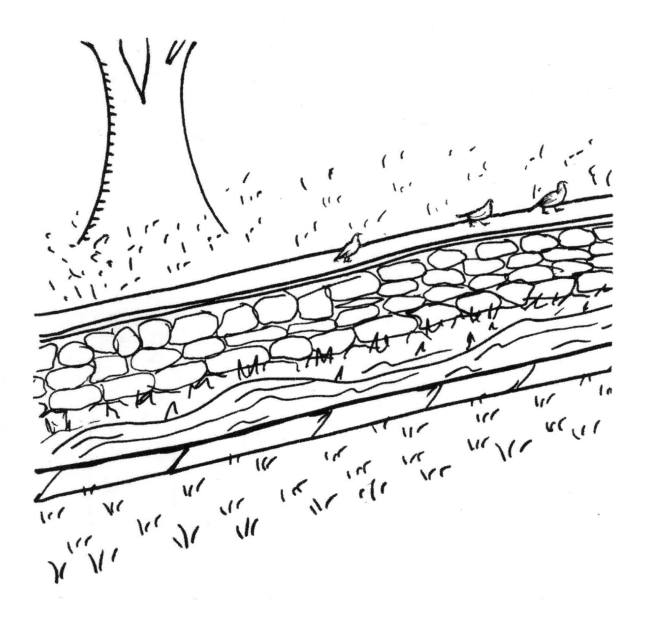

Bright **GREEN** grass grows in the park along the Santa Fe River.

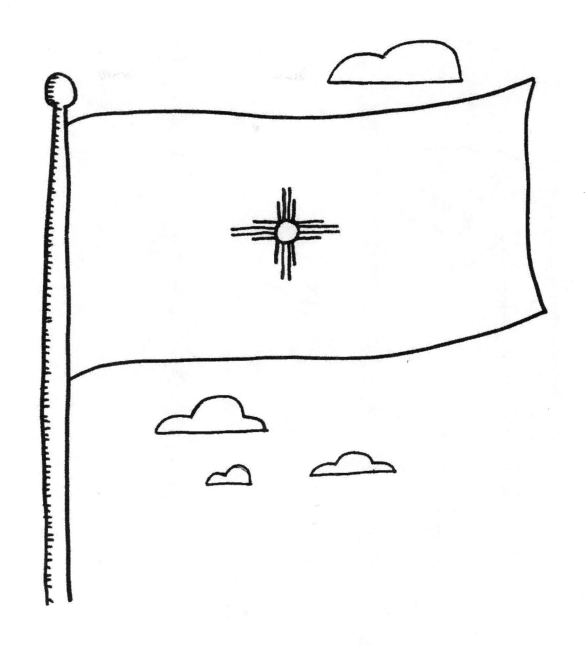

The **YELLOW** New Mexico flag waves in the wind.

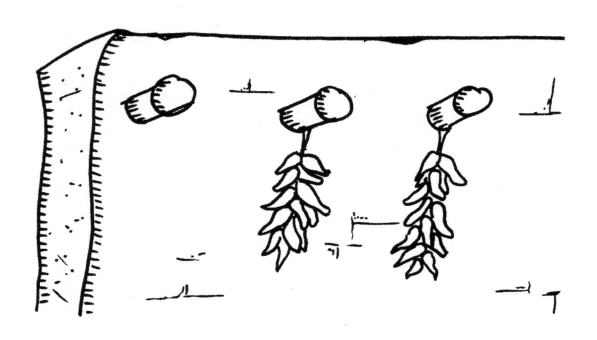

RED chile ristras
hang along adobe walls.

I pitch peanuts
to the pigeons in the **PLAZA**.

When the sun shines on their **GRAY**
feathers, I see flashes of color.

I see **INDIAN POTTERY** that is:

BLACK

 **WHITE**

BLACK and WHITE

I walk in front of the
PALACE OF THE GOVERNORS.

There I see beautiful **TURQUOISE** stones in **SILVER** jewelry.

In Santa Fe I hear **BELLS**

Bells high in the Cathedral towers
ring in the morning
and the evening.

In the oldest church, **SAN MIGUEL**,

I ring an enormous bell.

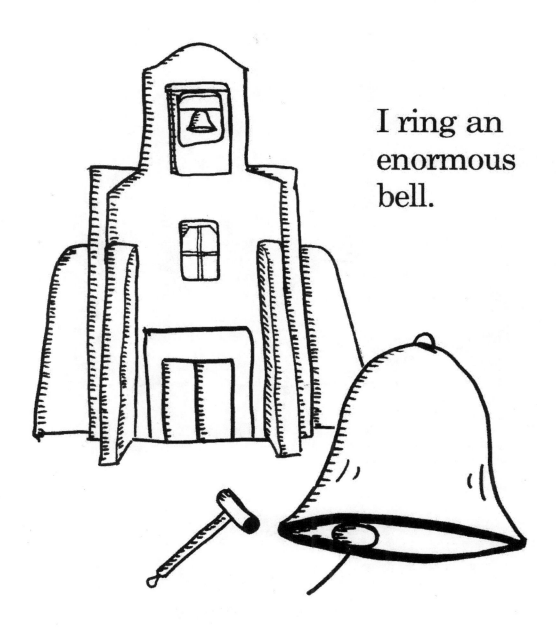

WATER

I hear water squirting and splashing from my favorite statues.

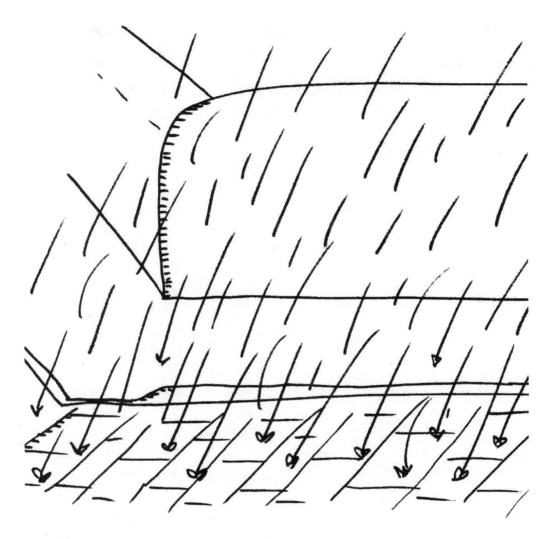

Raindrops plop, plop, plop on the wet pavement during a summer shower.

I hear water splish, splish, splash
in the **SENA PLAZA** fountain.

Sometimes I hear a little water trickle, trickle, trickle in the **SANTA FE RIVER**. Sometimes I hear a lot of water roar under the bridges.

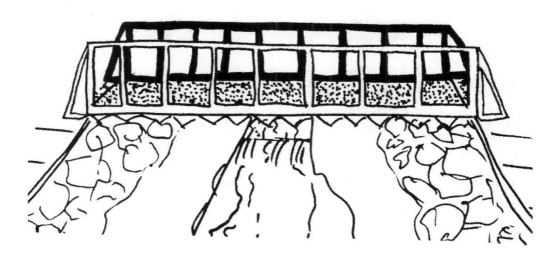

Sometimes I don't hear any sound from water in the river, because sometimes there isn't any water in the Santa Fe River!

In Santa Fe I taste . . .

PIÑONS

Piñon nuts grow inside piñon shells.

Piñon shells grow inside
piñon pine cones.

Piñon pine cones grow on piñon pine trees.

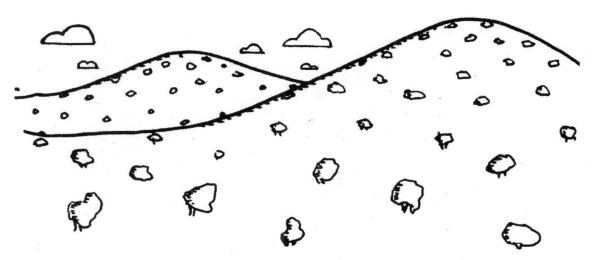

Piñon pine trees grow on the hills around Santa Fe.

TORTILLAS

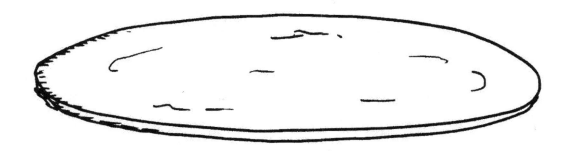

Tortillas are flat like pancakes.

Tostadas are toasted tortillas. I dip them in salsa. Hot chile! Hot! Hot!

Cooks wrap tortillas around other foods to make:

Enchiladas

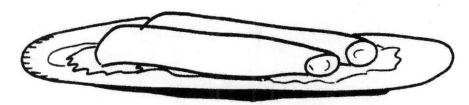

Burritos

Tacos

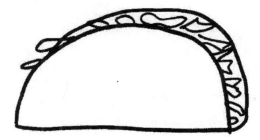

SOPAIPILLAS

Sopaipillas are like puffy little pillows.

I bite off one corner and pour in honey. Yummy!

ICE CREAM

After a busy day in Santa Fe I buy an ice cream cone.

I sit on a fancy iron bench in the Plaza, and lick, lick, lick, lick, slurp!

In Santa Fe I smell . . .

Cookies cooking

Bread baking

DELICIOUS SMELLS

Steak sizzling

PIÑON SMOKE

In winter
I smell the smoke of piñon wood
burning in Santa Fe fireplaces.

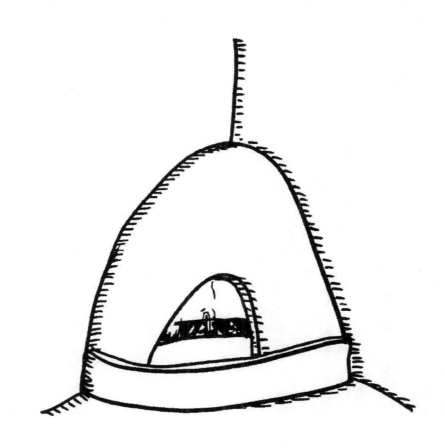

In summer the smell of piñon smoke lingers in some fireplaces. Can you smell it?

In Santa Fe I touch . . .

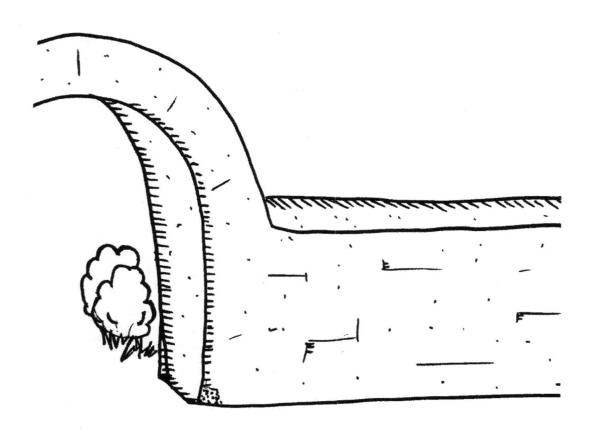

a **ROUGH** adobe wall, **WARM** from the Santa Fe sun.

A fence surrounds the monument in the middle of the Plaza. I touch the **SHARP** points on the fence. Ouch! Ouch! Ouch! I wonder if the point on top of the monument is sharp too?

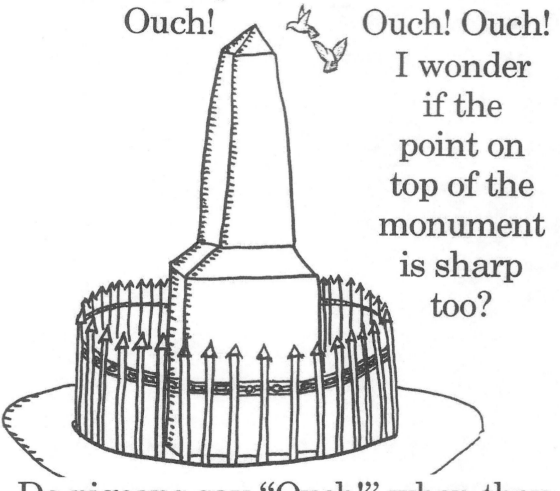

Do pigeons say "Ouch!" when they land on it?

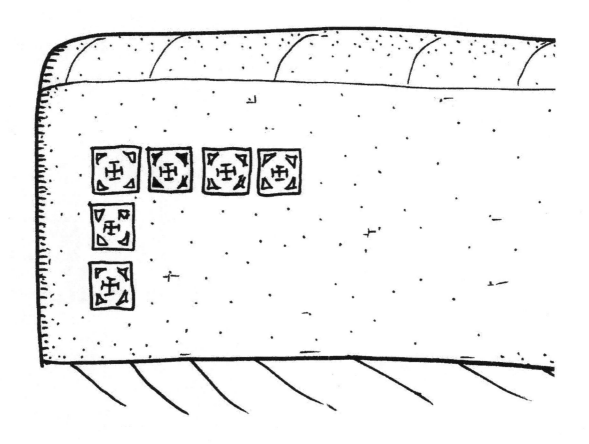

Colorful tiles feel so **SMOOTH**, especially when they are set in rough adobe walls.

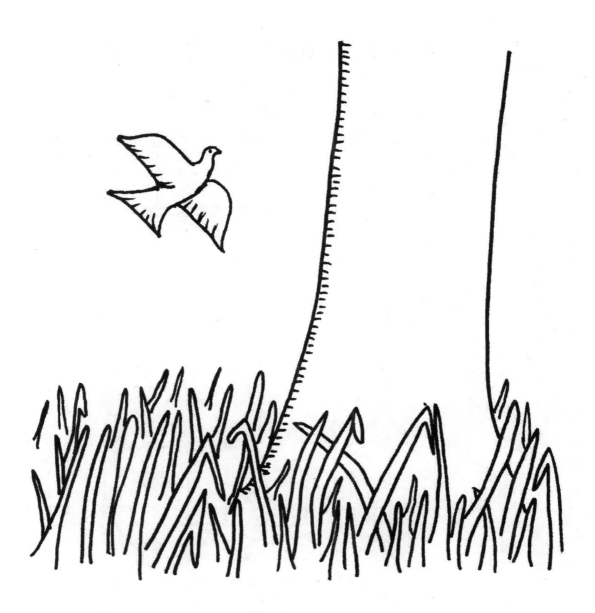

The grass under shade trees in the Plaza feels **COOL** and **DAMP.**

I touch the colorful rugs and blankets in Santa Fe. Some feel **ROUGH,** some **SOFT,** some **SMOOTH,** some **SCRATCHY.**

I feel the names of children carved in a walkway of bricks. These children helped build my favorite museum.

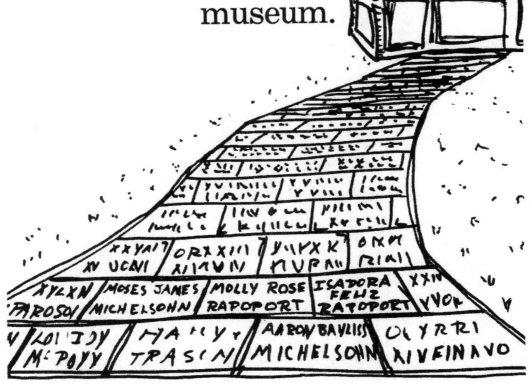

At most museums signs say "Do Not Touch". At the Santa Fe Children's Museum I can touch **EVERYTHING!**

THE END

THE AUTHORS

Libby Lynn is the childhood name of a grown-up author who wrote *I See Santa Fe!* with her son. It is her first book for children.

Moses James is the New Mexican boy who likes the wonderful sights, sounds, tastes, smells, and touches of Santa Fe. Pitching peanuts to pigeons in the Plaza (as well as chasing them) is one of his favorite pastimes.

The authors thank Larry Michelsohn, David Michelsohn, Alicia Chavez, and Welden Bayliss for their help in preparing this book.

Questions? Comments? 2LynnMichelsohn@gmail.com

You might also enjoy these books about Santa Fe written for adults by the author,
Lynn Michelsohn:

Billy the Kid in Santa Fe,
	A Non-Fiction Trilogy
Book One: Young Billy, Old Santa Fe
Book Two: A Confining Winter
Book Three: Chasing Quicksilver
		(coming soon)

Billy the Kid's Jail, Santa Fe, New Mexico

Made in the USA
Columbia, SC
17 September 2024

42463271R00020